BOUTIQUE BOOTCAMP

A Beginner's Guide to a Profitable Online Retail Store

Table of Contents

Introduction

You're ready to start your online boutique—but where to begin?!?

Boutique Bootcamp takes the guesswork out of starting your new online boutique. Launching any business is difficult, but online stores come with their own hang-ups. As a successful online beauty and fashion store owner, I have made ALL the mistakes. Determined to make it, I invested countless hours and money into paid workshops, books, and entrepreneurial classes. I spent all my time in online social groups trying to gather all the information I needed to succeed—and I did! Learn from my sweat equity and prepare for your success with such tools as:

- Naming your business

- How to choose quality items

- Strategies to keep up with demand

- Where to access fashion, beauty, and décor vendors

- Marketing, branding, websites, and more…

After reaching my goals, I knew it was time to share my wins and losses, hoping to help someone else reach theirs. Let me help you take the next steps.

Because until you spread your wings—you have no idea how far you can fly!

What Is Your Passion?

This question is critical because not every day will be a good one, so you want to start with something you're passionate about.

What comes easy to you that might be hard for others? Is there something you've done from an early age or that your family and friends have come to expect from you, and you don't give it a second thought? Finding your passion is less about what makes the most money and more about the individual talents and abilities you love! Once you've found that and have made a genuine connection with your ideal client or customer – the money will come!

Let's face it – there's competition out there, so it's important to find your "lane" and stick to it! Niches are a specialty that makes your boutique stand out from the rest. An area with noticeably clear and detailed boundaries, leaving no room for confusion. So, do you have an online clothing boutique that carries the latest fashions for plus-size women, or children's clothing with a specialization for newborns or preemies? What about wigs – but only braid, loc, or twist units? Have you always had "an eye" for putting looks together and thought nothing of it? Your online boutique could feature home décor or outfit ideas for those who may not be as gifted in that area. Deciding on what your boutique will carry and specialize in is important so take some time and think about what speaks to you, and who you are!

Whether you've decided to carry women's, men's, or children's clothing, bags, shoes, jewelry, hair, or home decor – make it something that you love! You are your own walking free advertisement showing your brand in the best possible light – so make it count!

When starting my business, I wasn't sure of the first steps to take but **Boutique Bootcamp** *gave me the confidence to get started and information I didn't even know I needed. The advice and guidance was clear and easy to follow. The first step to following your dreams is always hard, but this makes it a lot easier.*

- Anatasia Conyers, *Singing In The Rain, Inc.*

D.D. Laselle recognizes the hurdles and pitfalls in starting an online business and calls them out in this book. **Boutique Bootcamp** *helped me to avoid some of them and get on the right track with my business.*

- VaShon Revils, *Beautifully Braided Wigs*

Thank you for filling a void at an affordable price. Your book, **Boutique Bootcamp** *was just what I needed to get started and I received hundreds of vendors as a bonus!*

- T. Woodard

You have no idea how much time and money **Boutique Bootcamp** *potentially saved me. The way it breaks down the subjects – delivering them with clarity and simplicity helped me to begin making my dream a reality!*

- Linda Ellis, *Exclusive Events*

What Is Your Name?

You've decided on your passion, so what's the name of your boutique or business going to be? Your name should stand out and clearly state what your product or service is. It is often the first opportunity to make a good impression and should therefore be memorable. Think about – what you'll be doing, who you'll be doing it for, and what message or feeling you want your name to convey. In what way does your product or service benefit your client or customer? The answers to these questions will also help you come up with your bio (a clear and concise description of your business and what you offer delivered in 2 -3 sentences) which is invaluable.

Think of a few ideas and sit with them for a little while. Write them down and say them out loud to see which one feels best and sticks!

Once you've decided on your name, check to make sure it is available for new businesses with your local state agency, and for any state specific licensing requirements.

If you're not quite ready you can reserve the name in most states for as little $10.

Tip – Go to IRS.com and apply for your EIN number after you've secured your name and necessary licensing. It's free and you get it right away. You'll need this to open a business bank account (ALWAYS keep personal and business funds separate!) and to gain access to some of the vendors listed at the end of the book.

Who Is Your Target Audience?

Most often, our ideal client or follower is a mirror image of ourselves. Someone whose life or experiences you can relate to and would like to enrich through your products or services.

What areas do you have experience or expertise in? What group of people would benefit most from it?

What is their gender, age, ethnicity, religion, income or salary, and marital status? Do they have children? What are their political views, goals, challenges, and values? What are their hobbies and interests? What languages do they speak? How do they consume social media? What have they tried already that didn't work? When will they use your product or service, and why will they buy it? Is it a matter of convenience or a lack of knowledge and ability for them? Where do they live and shop? Are they most often impulsive shoppers or do they take more time to think purchases over?

Some of these questions may seem insignificant; however, the answers are directly related to who you market to and the best ways to go about it. If you have willing family and friends, conduct in-person interviews or setup an online poll to gather useful information.

Take some time to identify exactly who your ideal client or customer is.

Focus on the people, not just the product or service, and you'll get the template for a great and long-lasting connection.

Your Webpage

Having a reliable website and a great landing page is crucial. Decide exactly how you want your ideal client or customer to feel when they visit the site. Should the colors, print, spacing, and font lean towards feeling serious and determined or happy and enthusiastic as they browse through the pages? Elegant and classy or soft and whimsical? For example, if you've chosen to create a baby boutique, your color palette could feature soft blues, pinks, greens, and yellows with adorable baby giraffes and pandas. Whatever you decide, a clear and concise format, attractive colors, good images, and an easy-to-use platform go a long way in determining how long visitors stay on the site, and whether they ultimately make a purchase.

Also, be sure to include a solid "About Us" page. One of the top 10 most popular pages of a website is the "About Us" page. It provides a personal glimpse of the company and its owner. Potential customers or clients often choose a company they feel a connection to, so remember to be genuine and share the authentic you.

You can spend $100 or more and find someone on platforms like Fiveer or you can do it yourself on easy-to-use platforms such as Wix or Shopify. I've done it both ways and honestly both turned out well. One option costs more in money and the other in time – so it's up to you.

Tip – BUILD YOUR EMAIL LIST!

Invite all site visitors to stay connected by subscribing to your email list. This makes marketing a bit easier since you already have an active email list.

Your Images

The images on your site say a lot about you, your brand, and the products or services you decide to sell.

With your target audience in mind think about how your products or services should be displayed. Who will be the face of your brand? Will it be a logo or yourself? Will you use mannequins or models? Do you have any photogenic friends? Will you feature people at all or just the items and services? Keep in mind that there is no right or wrong answer here; it is about you, your brand, your target audience, and the message you are trying to convey.

If you have the budget to have professional photos taken, do it. BUT if you do not (I didn't), then portrait mode on an up-to-date iPhone works just fine. Be sure to pick a terrific location or background that accurately represents your brand, or you can keep it crisp with an all-white backdrop. Highlight the product or service you're selling from all angles; try to answer all the questions you might ask if you were the one making the purchase.

You can also get both free and pay-per-picture images from platforms like Pexels and Shutterstock. Just search your industry or specific business, and there are plenty to choose from. Keep in mind that you might see the free images on other same-industry sites; however, they are just fine to use by themselves or in combination with those you've taken.

Remember to choose images that are cohesive, speak to your ideal client or customer, and remain true to your brand.

Your Social Media

Social media can be a source of nearly unlimited information and can help you to connect with potential clients or customers who might otherwise be unreachable. The vast opportunity for growth here with just a few clicks cannot be ignored!

So, get your socials (Facebook, Instagram, TikTok, Twitter, Pinterest, YouTube, etc.) going as soon as possible, link them to your website, and be sure to include and do the following:

- Bio – This is your "elevator pitch." Describe you and your brand clearly and concisely in 2-3 sentences.

- Clarity - What does your ideal client or customer need to search for to find you? Make sure your Facebook / Instagram, etc., name, profile picture, and postings stick to your brand, niche, and the clients or customers that you serve.

- Consistency – Show up often and do it well through posts and stories. Ask questions and use hashtags. Engage daily, respond to comments, and provide value in your responses.

- Contact Info – Be sure to include your email and phone number, as well as the link to your webpage on all socials! Transparency and great customer service are still highly valued. Make sure that your clients or customers can reach you with questions or complaints.

- Creditability - Be truthful and authentic in your posts. Trying to be too much like someone else is tiring, and your customers will eventually see through it.

- Visit other social media pages often using your interests to find people, gain followers, and bring traction to your page.

Your Marketing

A good marketing strategy is key to any successful business, but you can also get lost trying to make it work, so don't over think it!

Remember that you are your best marketing tool, so know your company's bio inside and out. That means you can explain your business, goals, and who you serve clearly and without hesitation. Be honest and authentic.

- Find Facebook and Instagram accounts to follow that align with your boutique or the direction you plan to go. Be sure to like and comment on posts to get your name out there.

- Join Facebook entrepreneurs and local business groups. Ask and answer questions when appropriate. You never know what ideas or collaborations can come from introducing yourself, your business, and just being friendly.

- Use Facebook advertising, reels, and TikTok to bring attention to your brand and page. Be sure to engage with followers and answer any questions as soon as possible.

- If you have the budget use platforms like Fiveer for marketing images and logos that you need. If not, a $12.99 monthly subscription to Canva works fine for creating flyers, sales ads, etc.

- Conduct surveys. For example, put together two different outfit combinations using a few of your boutique pieces and survey which ones your followers like best to increase engagement.

- Host giveaways that require followers to tag and share your post three or four times to enter with a certain percentage off or to win a virtual gift card (generated code) as the prize. Don't forget to include an end date.

- Research influencers on YouTube / TikTok – contacting them about trying and promoting your brand.

- Require a post to be shared with five friends "who love shopping as much as you do, and you could win $25 off your next purchase!" Encourage them to subscribe now to….

- Ever done a Pop-Up Shop? It's fun and you meet new people while getting your name and brand out there! Find venues that are hosting events that complement your brand and purchase a table or host an entire pop-up yourself! You'll get your name out there, generate income from the sale of products or services AND connect with other vendors.

- Email Campaigns – Create a "Coming Soon" or "End of Inventory Sale", etc. flyer on Canva and use your email list to send it to anyone who has visited your site. Include a certain percentage off code for anyone taking advantage of the sale.

- Hashtag Trend – Find or start a hashtag relevant to both your industry, community, upcoming events, and your brand. Link it to your posts as well as meaningful comments on other well-established and relevant pages.

- Each day, find a hashtag relevant to your brand and comment on the first 15 photos.

- Identify 5 relevant hashtags and visit the top page of each, leaving a thoughtful comment on the top 5 posts.

- Network! Attend network events (virtually or in person) or host one yourself. Be prepared to exchange business cards (yes – they still exist!) and to talk about yourself and your business.

Your Inventory!

The included vendor list has hundreds of vendors including the ones that I used. Be sure to subscribe to their individual email lists so you'll receive new inventory and sale notifications!

If you've decided to carry clothing, make sure you have various sizes and colors in stock. The same goes for shoes; try to keep the average sizes stocked but carry a few of the unusual sizes too. For wigs, bundles, frontals, closures, etc., it's essential to stock varying lengths and colors. You want to be known for having a diverse and well-stocked inventory. However, be mindful of trends and make sure your purchases make sense. Avoid going overboard just because a vendor has a good sale; it can lead to having items that don't sell. Consider your storage space when deciding on inventory. Do you have enough space to store all your inventory, or would a drop shipping arrangement with the vendor be a better option for you?

When choosing items for your online store, make the shopping experience as easy as possible for the customer. If it's clothing, put entire outfits together and show them how your items can be styled. If you carry hair extensions or print T-shirts exclusively, pair them with complementary items to complete the look and help customers envision themselves wearing them. If you offer home décor services, create different room looks or bedding sets that customers might want to see in their homes.

When choosing vendors, read reviews to avoid potential headaches. Look for vendors with fast shipping and lower shipping rates. If they sell items in small enough quantities consider purchasing just a few to try out yourself and assess the fit, quality, etc., to see if they align with your brand.

Use the pricing formula below to calculate whether the vendor's asking price per piece is reasonable and offers a good profit margin. While the included vendor list is a great resource, be sure to do your due diligence in deciding which vendors and items work best for your boutique.

***Pricing Formula –**

$ per item (vendor price) + Individual shipping (shipping total divided by # of pieces ordered) = price you paid per item

Price you paid per item X 2 =?

? X .25 =?

Add the answer to the price you paid per item amount. Start your pricing at this amount and of course, always use your discretion.

Tip – Follow your favorite boutiques on social media, especially those that resemble your brand or where you hope to be in the future. If they have a particular piece that you like, consider purchasing it. Many of them source their items from some of the same vendors on the included list and sometimes they forget to remove the vendor's tag! I've discovered the sources of many of my favorite boutiques' pieces this way, and they often share vendors that you now have access to as well!

Afterword

Your reasons for wanting to start a boutique or become a successful entrepreneur may be different from mine but whatever the reason, remember that you can do this, and that "Nothing works for those who don't do the work."

Consistency is key! One day at a time - you've got this!

About the Author

"There's a ton of competition at ordinary, but there's almost none at extraordinary..."

D.D. Laselle is an accomplished entrepreneur, online fashion store owner, real estate investor, and debut author, whose book promises to be a valuable resource for aspiring entrepreneurs.

Originally from Virginia Beach, she earned a B.S. in business leadership from Old Dominion University in Norfolk, Virginia. She has since achieved success as a serial entrepreneur, with a diverse portfolio of accomplishments spanning various industries.

With a desire to help others find ways to succeed, D.D. has recently turned her attention to writing as a way of reaching many more people than she previously could. Her first book, ***Boutique Bootcamp***, uses her in-depth knowledge of this unique opportunity to take the guesswork out of starting an online fashion boutique and eliminate the mistakes she made as a newcomer so that new entrepreneurs hit the ground running.

Captivated by the art of storytelling, D.D. is currently penning her second book, a thoughtful blend of self-help and business insights, which promises to be just as enlightening.

D.D. has been happily married for many years and in her free time, she enjoys catching up with her adult children, traveling to new and exciting destinations, reading, and mentoring others in their quest for success. She is always thinking of new ways to improve her financial situation and devotes some of her spare time to helping single mothers and their children make better lives for themselves.

Her abiding aim in life is now to help as many people as she can to succeed, using her experiences of success and failure as a blueprint. She also plans to open a transitional home for single moms and their children at some point in the near future.

Vendors

Hernandez Sitemsing
Merci Collective

Gypsy Jazz
Silver Diva Jeans

Custom T Story
Lovervet

Bad Kiss
You Are Beautiful

Kool Katz
LFD

BenBen Apparel
PersonaliTees

Texas Toy Distribution
XCROWNS

Zim Designs
Loucia Clothing

CURVE DELICIOUS
Aeolus New York

Tulip Clothing
Anju Jewelry

Decozen
Sister Bees

Private Label by Velavida
Desden

Pivot Direct Inc
Funky Junque

Peking Handicraft
Paperfinch

Ampersand Avenue
Design

Vaan & Co.
Picnic Time

Adams & Co.
EnvyStylz

Go Charlotte
Rising International

Inner Beauty Gifts
Very G

Nu Steel
RainCaper

Tueba
Selected Fashion

Magic Fairy Candles
Aniise Beauty

PEACE AND DOZEN INC
That's So Andrew

Home Mart Goods
Inked Up Apparel

Tomoko House
Market Street Candle Co

Bianchi Candle Co
Shop Andi

Smells
1920

Azalea Wang

Perkies

Beettan

BAEZ

Classicharms

Street Level

Earth Song Jewelry

Zenara

Woman Runway Athletics

Sondra Roberts

Sistar Style

Khristee

BAIE BLEUE

Bazix

Hidey Style

Brunna Co

Natalie Mills

Wonderful & Young

Beyond Cushions

Evicto

TOUCH LA

Gypsie Jane

Good Feelings

Stylo

Luchiano

Visconti

Bringko

Augustine Hat Co.

Anne Cate

Northwest Designs

N Frequency

KENZKUSTOMZ

Signare USA

Print The Dream

Sport Leopard Chic

Chill

Queens Designs

Elle & Co

The Print Espresso

Watchitude

Pretty Bash

Tiepology

UVA Line

COCOA

Yes

Whet Blu

Evil Eye Favor

Vine Tree

The Wholesale Connect

Hanks Kerchiefs

Pretty Robes

Teegrams

RedMoon Collection

Laflare

Galita

Duckthreads

NOEUL + SIA

Coffee & Good Reads

DaydreamHQ

Vatchio

Ravello Intimates

The GOAT

1822 Denim

NotLabeled

Heyday

Do Take It Personally

Galore Home

Bholi Sage Plus

Eleven Point

Sunbeltgifts

Wald Imports

Send Me A Dream

Heart & Willow Prints

Dis Moi Lovely USA

Mapcie

Avoir La Peche

Memoi

Monhnny

Keniston

India Handicrafts

DILA

Begin Home Décor

Korissa

seven hearts shop

The New Class

Driftless Studios

Broken Top Brands

Lipstick Wholesale

Medusas Heirloom

Living Royal

Opal Road

Lucky Chuck

Statement Peace

Namaste Home

Lunabella Bracelets

Xela & Vic

BeBlessed

Hey Grl Hey

Jewelry Forever-Foxy

Liliana Shoes

Ivy Gold Co

Vibhsa

Belle's Design Shop

Vertigo

Southern Strut

Simran International Sterling

Kreek Vintage Life

Style Ensemble LLC

1st Allie

Zulay Kitchen

Wilco Home

Monkey Ride Jeans

Bella & Bear

C&E Design

Elana Kattan

SANJE WHOLESALE

Plutus Home Brands

Sky Jewelry

Debbie S Distributor

Shamarr Barquet

Kismet

Scrubs Collective

VBRT

Emerson West

Monfoot

A&B's Wholesale

Waitlist Accessories

Esmeray Clothing

The Elevated Abode

Cool Toolz

Prairie Fire Candles

Threaded Pear

The Dapper Paw

Beachables

Decorium Living

Ebru Home

Beauty Kitchen

Chic YC LLC

YAWOO GARMENTS

Cali 1850

Denise Albright

New Yorker's Apparel

Star Vixen

WonderXFans

Multitasky

Pink Machine

Willow + Grayce

Phantom Chef

Pizzazz

Nash Grey

Gray Bird

MKF Collection by Mia K

Miss Fancy Pants

Hart Denim

Glammy

Vintage Point

Doe A Dear

Dolma Inc

Kasih Co-op

Status Queen

Labe

PLine zone

SP Tops

Wilmax

England USA

Trendy Wholesale

T-shirts, Hoodies & More

Masutto

Venti6 Outlet

AVA Clothing

Vintage Blonde Tees

LA7

Public Goods

Freezia

ELJ Avenue

Petra Savage

Freeland Fashion

OBX Prep

VOSHAPE

EVA

Yura Clothing

Smoke & Mirrors

Hakan

Lashes4today

Cedar Crate Market

Mrkd For Life

Love Sock Company

See Rose Go

Runway Paris Design

Cotswold and Co

One N More Inc

LETTSGO

Young Threads

Rustic Raven Home Decor

Buy Socks You All

PopFun

Jade

Sister Fashion Inc.

Farah

Naz New York

Charmant

Ciel Choi Official

Cotton Foundry Wholesale

Abboo Candle Co

Saturday Skin

Banded

Swan

Madchen

Kona Active

Hollywood Sensation

Emma Grace Shoppe

Sassy nene

Barse Jewelry

Small Town Creations

Berek

A.C.G. Los Angeles

Raj Imports

Bandelettes

WildGrey

U Jeans

Cerule

Wild & Untamed Designs

Yoga Democracy

Mila + Stevie

Callie Lives South Beach

SMOKE RISE RED

Sole Star

Level Collection

A Deane Dream

Jupiter Gear

Aureum

Pehom

Tote&Carry

Harang

Istani

Blue Gem Sunglasses

Blue Planet Eco-Eyewear

The Greii

Wilder and Soul

Lunar Deer

Dreamer Jeans

Grey Violet Italy

Rebel Minds

BuyBuy Co

Got To Have It Fashion

Shady Lady

Amaryllis

Plush Appeal LLC

LAZYDAISY Swimwear

Lassiva Collection

Sofie the Label

Los Banditos

Urban Breeze

Mayes NYC

GetBullish

CG Habitats

Winsome Apparel

The Piggy Story

Vintage Canvas

Peach Puff

Lilac Sunset

Culture Code

Dong Sung USA

AFULY CAT

Eunoia Young Skincare

Lemonbella

ToTo Heros

KIMCINE

Woman Ocean

Sunkissedcoconut

De Sepreso

Ice Cream Life

Bouteeque Closet

BFF Footwear

Velvi

Something About You

Orange Poppy

Kushi-riki

Iconic Trade

Milly Belles

FlippySox

Switch Remarkable

Gyal Bashy

Lexi Hope

Nova Design

Trio Urban

La Mode N Co NY

Kreative Kale Co.

Urban Diction

Coin1804

Girly Empire Wholesale

PINKme

Va Va Voom

Hana By KWM

Screamer

Little Trendy

Bambu Apparel

Shuuk

Out With Grace

T.B.O.

Mabell

ClaudiaG Apparel

Tees2urdoor

By Jaidi

Peony Pastels

Color Theory

PASTEASE

Shoppingwill

Lavender J

Beauty Stash

Ricki Designs

Pinkcherry Inc.

Woolzies

White Stone Blue River

K-Fashion Swoop

Nette Road

OMSutra

Lazy Daisy

Uplifting Threads Co

Viva Maria

BULLTEES

Quotable Life

Wild Oates

Muche Et Muchette

Tip Top Kids

Nicole and Nia

Pure Drop

Meek

A Ellen

emproved

Fabulous Icon

Anna & Sarah

Harkaari

The Trend Apparel

Typically Blush

Southern Chic Wholesale

Malta collection

Bleached & Boujie

Brangio Italy

White Waves

BYRKA

MiiM

JadyK

The Stylista

BC Sport Shop

J.F. Designs

Willow + Alder

Cape Cod Chokers

Actus

Era Vanity

Smoke Apparel

SI Advance

Tapa Fashion

JC Sunny Fashion

J. Her

Ensemble

Alan Pendergrass Robes

Retail Security Store

TFY Collection

Innominate

Mangosteen LA

VAVITHO

StashCart

Pop Cutie Inc.

Klesis

Mehers

The Label

Pure Spa Gifts

BILA

Aubrey Kathryn Co

LA Color

The Classy Cloth

Lemonade Shoes

Azura Stratus

CartoonUSA

Glance Apparel

Poetic Justice

Everina

Prima Dress

Kathaya

The Juniper Shop	POP TOY
WFFS	My Young Fashion
Select Apparel	Generation Zillionaire
Stylive	YNEZ
Heavens Earth Shoes	Eevee Leggings
Nocturne	Silvergate
BD Lasers, INC	RAMI
ESW Beauty	Dionee
Standards & Practices	Orchid Bloom
SF Fashion	Solar Eclipse
The Hat Depot	Knours
Camel Threads	Atlas Goods
Pure Print	Levelle
Ravesuits	Leena
NEOCLASSICS	MERIGOLD KISS
Charming Bunny	Kingdom And State
UP CLOTHING	Six Point
Fashion World	Hollis Haley
AIBLEE	GLAMBAE FASHION
Beyouty Inc	Aluvina
BEE-OCH Organics	Cotton and Crate
Levu	Million Colors
Inner Beauty	Beivy
Ellie Rose	SimKai Shoppe
Edgar's Bath Goods	Wholesale Dress Outlet
LUELLE	M3 by Monica
Kaktus Sportswear	Ariel USA

VAV NEW YORK

Lovesome

United Lovers

B Sydney

Style Up

LUXYUSA

Annemomo

Lawrence & Company

KINdom

FAFB Apparel

PGF

LOVBAG

SOLOVE

Shallot Collection

Rockledge Designs

Jill's Jewels

Alamia

Mica Denim

EMMAUS.INC

Lucca Couture

spice rose

Bleached Tie Dye

Villa Bain

Chic N Go

Apex Canyon Apparel

SurelyMine

Multifaceted

Things Between

Cherry Cloth

BUTTERMELON

Love Lina

Zopali

Glass Two

Fashion In The Box

Cosmic Skates

Wenbo International Trade

AnnieWear

Aly Rose

Howlpot USA

Dainty Delights Creations

Elite Jeans

LAPCOS

Ceros Jeans

LaLaSista

Pennys Purses

Moda Sky

Aced It Apparel

CHIC STAR

Lovelulubell

Me O My Earth

The Curve LA Plus

Donna Di Capri

Sew In Love

Kanji Couture

PEACH MOOD

Fifty Pennies

J&J

Sparkle & Marble

8Apart

Pristine Wear

Aemi + Co

Enterprise Crossing

Wolf Whistle

Zollie

TrendyFive

Southern Elegance Candle Company

Chasing Portland

Dairi

Hersy Hanabee Boutique

Babe With A Dream

La Moda Clothing

Cowgirl Roots

Top Avenue

MyStyle Wholesale

Honestee

PPEPPI

POLY USA

Top Tier

Made With Love

Not So Plain Jane Design Co

Flarix Corp

Love Is All

Zoey Simmons Jewelry

day + moon

Freeme

Tabbisocks

Queen

Miss Q Baby

Crave Body Jewelry

One And Only Clothing

Lane Seven Apparel

Vice Edition

Pinktown USA

Eterna

Love Mist Accessories

Akalia

OnTrendForLess

OASISINCENTIVES

Rag Company

ANTI NOBODY

Gold Elite Apparel

Bella

Litz O.Vianca

AmoJewels

Noire Handbags

Present And Love

Lychee Blanco

Ruby May Cosmetics

Pine Apparel

Sifides

Petalo

LA RENTA FASHION

La Hammam

Saved by Grace Co.

Cocoboo Accessories

Amellia

Terani Couture

Qwasabee

Perfect Shape

Tres Bien

Fourttunata

Lovestrength

It's A Henry

Bangle and Babe

DesignerBrandsForLess

ShowStopShoes

Fashion Space

ArtcareShop

Fancy Dream USA

Up Sportif

Stylish Swimwear

Jade By Jane Plus

LA LUXE

LeggingGirl

Kolorspun

Dora Landa

Crazy Heifers

Opposite Sense

Lattelove

8 CORE

Petal Dew

Parker Jeans

TITO BIDA

Timeless Tees Shop

Love Susie

AF Design Group

San Francisco Umbrella Company

Mark Jenkins Footwear

Love and Repeat Clothing

CHW

HESPERUS

LALAVON

Marrakech Shop Design

Le Reussi

Betsy Moss

Barrel Down South

Most Wanted USA

7DAYS SOCKS

Verae

Pure Style Girlfriends

SOONIPOUCH

First Row

Elizabeth's Fashion

TheSnugSuit

JANUARY 7

Tasha Apparel

bead & bond

Mistyrose Skyiley

BOB BROWN

Mini Pocket

Epoch Hats SHIKU

FootClothes

SONG4U

Jacquie the label

Evolve Botanica

Elleborn

Ellison and Young

K&L International

SOS Bliss

Endless Love Fashion

DDK Footwear

Set & Stones

ZinoVizo

Crunchy Diva Designs

Pixie Apparel

My Life Apparel

Luxe Wear

J.OUR

Kompanero

THA Dressing

Cell Lab America

N By Nancy

Lola Jeans

PETRA153

Edgeu Nail

BSL

LA Society

ASA Clothing

Smilende Co.

Ivy and Sage Market

Esttia

La Roseason

24-7 Daddyhood

REVEROF

DOTCOM

Love and Thyme

Everlynn

The Light Bag Co

Rosa Clothing

Mer St Barth

Studio66

ReeBees

PINK NABI

COLORING YOU

Neon Bohemians

Yabes

Kimbrose

Wisteria Lane

Marvy Gal

NCURV

Maude Mode

Eye Candy LA

Wrapped. By Sav

Monkey Wave

BOBOS Remi

Truffle Soda

Modern Haze

Brenda Grands Jewelry

Karma and Luck

Mermaid Swimwear

Sugarfox

Crunchy Love Co

Magnolia Fashion Wholesale

Cheryl Creations

Limitless

Alesia Designs

ZAMONG

Frem

Ozone Socks

Medy Jewelry

Anna-Kaci

Glister

DOBBI N3 Decor

Knobs

Ellie Dog Wear

Denim Love

Jelly Jeans

Urban Savage

mi cielo

Blue Turtle

MULLA

Graphic Addict

TIME AFTER TIME

T-Shirt Snob

KloudBambu

Caterpy

Moon Ryder

OMG Styles

SOCALI

Immediate Apparel

Black Pearl Clothing

KAXI

Wild Lilac

ClaudiaG Collection

Two 12 Fashion

Future Brands

Cait + Co

Golden Rose Co

Mimosa

Elloh

Tiana Designs

AHJOEAH

Hannah Amazon Baby Wear

Maker's Shoes

Sparkling Pieces

Brown N Sweet

Girl Nation

Lauren Lane

Anais Bella

Small Town Society Apparel Co

Katie May's Place

Simple Heart Co

Doshi

Fini

ALAMAE Apparel

White Splash

LYON Luminaries Candle Co.

26 International

Tyes By Tara

208 Tees

Mod Miss Jewelry

FASHION PARADISE

Joe K Inc.

Miracle

WUDN

Makeup Junkie Bags

ZIA Eyewear

SLEEPAHOLIK

Splendid Iris

THE FOUTA SPA

Buddha Pants

Daniel Jeans

Lily Gray

Organic Generation

JHP Collection

LIME MIST

Avenue J

BLING TEES

LIME ALL THE TIME

OTOS Active

ToeSox

IBstylish

BHANTI

Davoir

Angels Welcome Market

Annva USA

Bo Bags

Wootie

Dresses By Lily

Stamps Creative Design

Itssy Inc

Leetie Lovendale

Young Socialites Clothier

PinchMe

Life Clothing Co

Mayor Clothing

Spiffy & Splendid

5 Game Face Team Shop

TODAY FASHION

Tropical Blossom

American Threadz Apparel

Beachcomber Footwear

Oli & Hali

Samantha Margaret

GJG Denim

Zion

SAMAS FOOTWEAR

Green Tree Jewelry

Daphne Lo

Zam

SKY PLUS

Smart Mouth Threads

Modern + Chic

After 12

Mira Luxe

Mattie and Mase

Amy Lynn

All Moments

Bizfete

On You

Jovee

KikiSol

Shoe App

ROSEMEAD LOS ANGELES CO

Illustrated Society

BJD Inc.

People of Leisure

Love Bubby

Licosa Group

XoKendallCo

Boss Babe Collection

A Girl's Gotta Spa!

Grace in LA

SMOKE RISE

D and E Tees

Signature 89

KC Factory

Stitch Lane

Asamo

Katydid

Dixie Grace

Peace Love Fashion

Threads Wholesale

Oooh Yeah Socks

Still Friday

Cape Robbin

MARS SKY

TOP WOMAN

LA Pop Art

Rustee Clothing

D'liteful

Tropic Like It's Hot

Kids by Kissed Apparel

Aili's Corner

Viv & Lou

Ziba Apparel

MOODPJMS

Tua

Coterie Closet

Hustle+Heart

Urban Rose

Sweet Adelyn

Julia by Love J

4 POLAR BEE

Southern Bliss Company

Thomas and Lee Co

LLD Supply

J-Slips Hawaii

Hope Horizon

Bellissima Fashion

Honeypeach

Rokoko Love

MIA Accessories

Ranee's

Summer Creek Apparel

MOVENDU

AKCE Jewelry

Sweet Lemon

Jordan Taylor

BESTON

Popsi Lingerie

HRT&LUV

FemFetti

Miss V Collection

Just Me

Wild Lucille Apparel

Dylan Jewelry

I TOO

The Celie Timber

Oak Candles LLC

Fadcloset

Sunday Brunch

MIOU MUSE

CLICK PUFF

OOPS!

Shoplobbie

Mad for Love

ROOLEE

JSQUAD CLOTHING

Edit By Nine

Sky To Moon

1clique co.

Olive and Ivory Wholesale

ANWND

Poison Mushroom

Lemon Lorraine's

CREATE X5

ONE & ONLY PLUS

The Ancient Bazaar Jewelry

Summer 10 Magazine

Bacon Lettuce Tomato

OMG Blings

Willow & Grace

CLR Wholesale

Annes Apparel

Voy

GM GLOBALENTERPRISE INC

Control Apparel

Shopin LA

Millibon

Jaylanie

Julia Rose

Headbands of Hope

Aviano

LYL FOREVER INC.

S-SISTER

Kids Charm Online

Fox and Owl Apparel

Rain Wear

Ombra USA

Machu Picchu Jewelry

CO-PACK INC

Nina Rossi

2BME FASHION

MNI Los Angeles

Loverly Fit

MABLE

Pretty Garbage

Divine Apparel

JNL Selection

BENIE

Blue Codine

SHOPNEIGHBORS

Kbeautynet

shoeroom21

Adorable Sweetness

Dessin Studio

Letter to Juliet

Hanmi

Protech Inc

GYAHN CLASS

Sorrelli

HANTON INTERNATIONAL GROUP INC

BESTTO

Dexire

Oneleven

Shamaim

L2C Fashion Studio

HONEY TEE

You Bronze

Funky Monkey Fashion

YOUMI

Jackie London Inc

Feel in

Alexis G

To Star

NVIU

Dani & Em

Sweet Lover Fashion

Perfect Peach

NoBrand

Canvas Apparel

Kentce Fashion

Crover

PAPARAZZI by BIZ

Lady Curvaceous

Adele B

Orange Farm Clothing

Chanour Jewelry

DAVENDU

EL Kanna

OLLA BELLA

Holindang

RORY

MintChoco

Another Mode

Bluevelvet

ZANNZA Couture

Handbag Factory

Jesse&J

Fashion Fantasia

Sewn and Seen

Blue S

Shoe La La

Allium

KARA USA

On Blue

Jack and Jill

Retro Fashion

Annice

Palomares Apparel Inc.

A3 Design

Nothing but Sexy

LENA

Jupiter & Me

Sundayup

REDLEAF FASHION INC

Queens, INC

The Care Collective

MG Clothing

TREASURE

Rolypoly

Heart and Arrow

Doro

LIKHA

Surf City Imports

Oopsie Daisy

Shelly Clothing

Brand Q

ePretty

Enriko Fashion Shoes

Lazypants

No Vacancy

Bella Chic

Jen & Co

O8 Lifestyle

The Burlap Bag

Tiri Pro

Two And Crew

Yira

ELODIE

Red Clover

MONACO FASHION

Chicways

Rollasole

G MINI

The Farming Artist

ENVME

BOOM BOOM JEANS

Kanari B

Zero Degrees Celsius

Best Underwear

RelieveIt

Jacaranda

Fine and Clear

Spikes and Seams

Excused

Shop Michella

SYMPHONY

BE WICKED

Primi

August Apparel

Melrose with Love

The NuVintage

Love and Repeat

NIKKI SMITH DESIGNS

AMOLI

Lovest

Hidden Brand

4 Duulce Intl

Lele For Kids

Amita Naithani

Sharon's Closet

Ask Apparel

Sweet Girl

Modern Opus

Fiesta Fashion

Perseption

Choice

Melie Bianco

@Balance

4 B Mine

Bailey Rose

Tyche

BLUME AND CO.

Thinkable

UPTOWN

YMI Jeanswear

FACETORY

Good Works Make a Difference

Luxe & Leather by Madonna & Co

Denim Zone

Nostalgia

Sweaterland

Mona B

ZiA Apparel

Z&Co.

La Diosa

Taba

Asher and Olivia

Rescued Wine

Midwest Tees

Things UnCommon

CAMEO

MA CHERIE Collection

MOJO USA

AMITIE

David & Young

Dirty Bee

Calison Inc

Pastel Design

ZAD

Qupid Shoes

CoolcrystalsInc

Miss Sparkling

Oat Collective

ACCITY

French Kiss

Lizush

Popular 21

Seriously Shea

BE A

Icon Sports

Whiteroom

Cactus Fancy Fashion

Rosevelvet

Lotus Fashion Collection

Thread Fix

GIBIU

Maven

BucketList

Kreamy NYC

Like Dreams

Magia AIMAMA

Malibu Sugar

America & Beyond

Jade By Jane

Cedar and Cypress Designs

Flint J.

PRINCESS GABREILA WHOLESALE

ACOA

Kollecte

Truly Contagious

Rowdy Crowd Clothing

Charming Shoes

HANA JEANS

StyleKorean

337 BRAND

Scents of Europe Distribution

MEDIHEAL

URBNIQUE

HauteMess Clothing

Almost Famous

REBODY

RIVIR

Finchberry

Lucylou Collection

mulawear

Leebrick

Excelsior

Insane Gene

A Quiver Full

Prince Peter Collection

Gipsy Queen

Piero Liventi

Whispering Willow

My Land

KOCOSTAR

Vibe Sportswear

Chloe Laetitia

TOPCOS

Pearlle

moodie

UNPLUG SOY CANDLES

Live Life Clothing Co

HaruHaru

Sweet habit

Noble Mount

Bellanova

Cottage Garden Bath

Pure Aura

ILLord Couture

Bighit Fashion

Generation XYZ

Enti Clothing

Apparel Candy

Avani Del Amour

Yellowcake Shop

Top Crate Clothing

STORY TELLER

Rambling Rose

Nodagi Fashion

Baubles by B

4 Naked Zebra

Last Call et clet

Sparkle Victoria Accessories

Purse Plus

THE M.A.P. JEANS

Bogue Milk Soap

DOGMA

Christie

Kaylee Kollection

Denim Lab USA

KIWI

The Jewelry Junkie

Live Love

Kidish

Joy Kids

iiShii Designs

Jessie Liu Collection

ING Athletics

SHEWIN INC.

Kind Lips

OOH SHOES

Karmela Cosmetics

Emerson and Friends

High MJ

3VERY

Mimozzas

Fabina

Valentine

Solo Giovane

Sissymini

Shop My Boutique

MP Apparel

One Spirit

Not Rated

nalgae wing

Greensky Cosmetics

EPTM

New Vintage Wholesale

Crystal Breeze

YAY NOVELTY

JayVee Kids

Self Contrast

Fashion City

SopranoLabs

Before You

Kimberly C

SORI

Type A Tees

DASH FORWARD WHOLESALE

Stay Warm in Style

Cotton Candy LA

WKNDER

YAK & YETI

Baci Fashion

Amici

Miss avenue

Unik

Something Special LA

Supreme Fashion

Votique

CIEN

FREYRS Eyewear

CAITE

Good Luck Tee

In The Beginning

Port 213

Cezele

MGM FASHION LLC

ROKOKO

Purple Candy

Coalition LA

OLIVE MAUVE

FASHIONEMOJI

Bella Closet

J.NNA

Fashion Nana

Avery Apparel

Urban Shoes

BURGUNDY APPAREL

CREPAS

MineB

Risen Jeans

Blue Buttercup

shero

Painted Threads

Heyson

Cecelia Designs Jewelry

LAmade

Eva Franco

Saints and Hearts

Gerard Cosmetics

Crescent

Rebel Stitch

Wildberry Waves

KKE Originals

Endless blu

Livana

Clear Color Shop

Celavi

Thistle and Clover

Amadi

TheRiver by JTW

Tina+Jo

Benares USA

Pleione

Half Heart

COMECO INC

SHIYING FASHION

Pretty Simple

MAZIK

TRESSER

Bluivy

Blanc

Justin Taylor

Lana Roux

Episode

Melon Fashion

Rose N Mary

P & ROSE COLLECTION

OCEANUS

Mine and E&M

Cloud Ten

Miss8

MACARON

Curvy Lovey

Kissed Apparel

Lola Paris

IF SHE LOVES

URBANARTEEZ

SOTD FOOTWEAR INC

FOLLOW ME APPAREL

What's Hot Jewelry

Ninexis

Mare Mare

SIWY

Adelyn Rae

Label + Thread

Saachi

Joh Apparel

STIVALI NEW YORK

Gretty Zueger

The Vintage Shop

Wall To Wall

For all seasons

JBD

Great Smoky

Lovesong

Fashioning Free as a Bird

Matty and Lux

Alphabet Apparel

Better Be

RK Apparel

LaBijou

The Immediate Resource

Dress Day

Lucy Paris

Charmo

Be Cool

G Stylez

Leia&Co

Cream N Sugar

SUNDAY MORNING

Ethan & Joy

LYDIA USA

The Sang

Sans Souci

Junie

HEIMISH

Haptics

Grace Your Style

Sexy Couture

ALPHIA

Winslow Collection

My Bump

MARINA WEST SWIM

CEFIAN

Neo Blue

Olive and Leaf

SELF CRUSH

PINCH

5 BaeVely

Cramilo Eyewear

Sweet Rain

Kay Kay Fashion

Cacelin Swimwear

MAZEL

Appleblossom

Coral Reef Swim

Dayday Fashion

SHOE ADDICT

I Fashion

Top Style

One and Only Collective Inc

Hemisphere Worldwide Sales Inc.

Pink Ripple

AND THE WHY

Cinderella Divine

Blush BJ

4 Shop Basic USA

Trending Times

Cali Boutique

24-HR FASHION

Arthur Jane Claire LLC

LUCKY PLANET

ORANGE USA HS INC

Her Bottari

Bonnie Bianca

PRIVY

Oista

Heimious

Ete Rose

No Less Than

miroh

CHICPIER

KATHMANDU IMPORTS

The Way

Labanby EVA

Insignia Footwear

Clover Cottage

Wona Trading Inc.

SALTY

Missfit

Find me Plus

Seduction L.A.

GTOG

idem ditto

Jenny Bean

Jvini

JUST USA JEANS

Reflex

Princess Purse 2

FSL APPAREL

Blue B 4

Judson & Company

Soxnet

RAD FASHION SM WARDROBE

Veveret

Avenue Zoe

Poppy & Plum

Hayden Plus Leaders Cosmetics

Eldridge

Athina

J2 FASHION

IN LOOM

Capricho

MDC International Inc

Ellie Flora

Anavia

Displaytown

ZIMEGO

Hailey apparel

Nic & Jo

Plain Apparel Tees

Mixologie

In2You

Regenbogen

La' Ros HOUSE OF LORDS RODEO CLOTHING

Amerikan Basics

Balboa Fashion

BiBi

Oily Blends LLC

MYS Wholesale Inc

8TH OF LA

Pinwheel

LANY Style

LIPPY CLIP

Anymore Jeans

Allie Rose

Spring Haze

Junk N The Trunk Tees

Sace

Magic Curves

EG fashion

Style Rack

Veracci

Milk & Honey

Belita Collection

THML CLOTHING

Aaron & Amber

VERVET by Flying Monkey

Wild Diva

Ricarica

Jane + One

Lesebi

Mary Clan Inc. Ole

FASHIONISTAR

Lenovia

Case Factory USA

Q2 US Jewelry House

FASHION EMPORIO INC

FANCO

By Claude

Venti6

Phil Love

Anarchy Street

Lovoda

Panache Accessories

All Row

XYNC Clothing

Kyemi

Vine & Love

ark & co.

Judith March

Hashttag Mystree Inc.

Rae Mode

LUV Fashion Shoes

Sweet Generis

Light So Shine

Dance and Marvel

SALT

Muselooks

Lake Flower Fashion Inc.

Spin USA

Day G

Isabella Chantel

Lush Clothing

Nature Denim

L&B Life

Fantastic Fawn

CAPSULLE

Final Touch

Lovely Melody

Sunnie LA Lily Clothing

Reveuse

Grade and Gather

Woven Pink

SHOP17

La Miel

See and Be Seen

Sapphire O

C'est Toi

Boswell

Fashion Blue Leopard

HOPELY

Il Bianco

LA Soul

Newbury Kustom Bombshell Bath

HONEYCAT Jewelry

TULIP.B

Happy Days USA

DS Wholesale Curve Market

Why Dress

Polagram

Dress Code LA

Blumin Apparel

Haute Fox

White Birch

I&M JEANS USA by Itzme

Hidden Jeans

5 TONY MARY

Voila	Perruzo Ent.
De Runway Footwear	Fashion District
GiGiO	Hesed
AAAAA FASHION	Bozzolo
Origami Fashion Inc	Glittering South
Miss California	Caviar Dremes
CCOCCI	Oddi Plus
SPECIAL A JEANS	AKAIV
Ariella	Blue Age
Plaza Mall	Ocean and 7th
BOMBOM	Luna
December Shoes	Chocolate USA
Love Sense	Main Strip
Vintage Soul	PINEAPPLE Beauty
MEBON	Salon de bebe
ENCORE JEANS	Caramelo Trend
Soul Thread	Boho Love
Pink4You	Seduzione
EINII	Rosio Clothing
Current Air	The Free Yoga
Honeydew	TSF Design
ASPEED STORIA	HiFashion
Avenue Hill	ILLord
Just Kids	Janette Plus
Joberry Accessories	May Blue
Strut & Bolt	Anny's Bridal
Hammer Collection	JJ's Fairyland

Miami Shoe Wholesale

Shark Eyes

Nicole Lee USA

Cinderella Couture

Tracie's 2010

TwentyTen

7th Ray

RESIDENTS ON

Midnight Proposal

Zutter

Miss Circle

Cherie Los Angeles

Cherry Mellow Inc

Twenty Second

Style U

a.gain

Many Many

Renee C.

2sable

Color Alien

Sassy Bling

Plus Size House

LA3accessories

Topping

Cutie Patootie Clothing

LITZ LA

Fashion Express

Acting Pro

Piboo Studio

Shoe Shoe Train

Blu Pepper

COCO Wholesale New York

Hailey & Co

FATE INC

Melrose Styles

Innocence

CJ Shoes

Toby Boys

Omega Trading

Dress Forum

Daniel K

Les Amis

Dazz

Suzie Q

Illa Illa

Miss Love

Renamed Enjean

Fore Collection

ePretty

Hers & Mine

Kid's Dream

Selini New York

Win Win Apparel

Vibrant M.i.U

Color Bear

Hello Miz

Vision

Namatt Design Pro

Hot & Delicious

Lucky & Blessed

Mod Ref

Sweet Lovely by Jen

Denim Couture

Hayden Los Angeles

Makers of Dreams

Knittrend

CY Fashion

Lady's World

On Twelfth

2 Hearts

Lux Los Angeles

Space 46

Quarter to Five

First Love

JW Signature

Focus Footwear

Aakaa

Rock N Rose

Red Ribbon

SKIES ARE BLUE

Codigo

TOP CHIC

Ellie and Kate

Beach Joy Bikini

Fashion Wildcat

By Together

Lovely J

New Trend On

Pixi and Ivy

Your Fashion Wholesale

Zenobia

Clothing of America

Must Have

Envya

P.S. Kate

Machi Footwear

Urban Fitz

Lovely Day

Sassy Look

Fun2Fun

ADORA

First Look

Cotton Bleu by Nu Label

Staccato

Got Style

Melody

Upmost

Caramela

Boutique Only

Fly Kidz

Blue Blush

Angry Rabbit

Levee

GLS Collective

Capella

Hem & Thread

Miley + Molly

5.00 Wishlist

Wanna B

Emory Park

LATISTE

Easel

YOOMOO

HAWKS BAY

Jodifl

143 Story

Listicle

dee elly

Bagel

ShopWTD

En Creme

LE LIS

Red Lolly

H&H Fashion

LUXXEL

Davi & Dani

Cello Jeans

BE Stage

Sugarlips

Lime 'N' Chili

Verte

Nylon Apparel

Machin Fashions

LOVE IT

Aphrodite Jeans

Machine Jeans

Tea & Cup

BANJUL

SJ Style

SHE

Mittoshop

Bonita Cosmetics & Accessories

Andree by Unit

Isac Trading

Avvio LA

Peach Love California Dreamers

Blandice Jewelry

Essue

Maronie by LAMR

Reborn J

Rousseau

Dorcas

G1K

Il Capriccio

Virgin Only

Beeson River

TIC TOC

Maniju Fashion

Hera Collection

Paper Crane

Oddi

Color Story

A Beauty by BNB

Kori America

Emma's Closet

12PM By Mon Ami

Charlotte Avery

Sweet Claire

A. Peach

Lumiere

POP Fashionwear

MUSA

Jireh Clothing

Jostar

Tea n Rose

Victoria Fashion

Good Girl

Artini Accessories

Urbanista

Esley

Ces Femme

INA

Wasabi + Mint

Vanilla Bay

HYFVE

CALISTA

H and R Costume Jewelry

Lancer's Fashion

O2 Denim

talent PLUS

Double U

Janette Fashion

Lovestitch

ICCO ACCESSORIES

IJOAH

Gilli

H&D Accessories

Leyva's

D.ROCK

Dear Prudence

OVI

Merveille

Mark Ashton Wholesale

American Bazi

Red Fox

Cielo

Funteze

M. Rena

RedShoeLover

Chatoyant

Docela

My Closet

Kan Can USA

K Too

Solution

Beloved

Rehab

Bella Berry

Catherine K Collections

Papermoon

Andrea Bijoux

Bear Dance

My Story

Fame Accessories

OhYes Fashion

Queen Mania

Emerald Collection

Heart & Hips

Doe and Rae

Sabora

Flying Monkey

5Besties

Sung Light Clothing

Yelete

1 Funky

BLOOMS IN THE CITY

Naked Zebra

Shine Imports Shampoo

Cozy Co

Verona Collection

H2K Trading

SONG AND SOL

Cemi Ceri

L.A Shoe King

Michel

S&J

Ocean and Land

Bag Boutique

Trinity Tribe

Beautysis

Let's See Style

Promesa

Apple Tree Apparel

Love In

S&G Apparel

Leto Accessories

TREND SHOP

LA Jewelry Plaza

Soieblu

Girly

ART BOX

B-Tween

Steven ELLA

Awesome J

Ambitiion

Anzell

Young 11 Fashion

Trendology Inc

Leggings Mania

SHOPIRISBASIC

CollectiveRack

IDEA

Loving People

Daisy Corsets

Apple B

Too Too Hat

Trendy Dress

VERY J

Apple Accessories

Bus Stop

Kova

TOP 10

Cap Zone

Olivaceous

BABYFOX

LA Hot

GeeGee

Ama Global

Uni Hosiery Co., Inc

Beulah Style

Trend Notes

Judy Blue

Faith Apparel

Stella Shoes

JW Designs

Ellison

The Moon

Karen T Design

Madelyn

Lemon Tree

Color 5

POL

Poliana Plus

Cezanne

Dilworth Road

CLOUDWALK

New Moa

CQbyCQ

Flying Tomato

Love Tree

Dynamic Fashion

Olive & Pique

Fascination

One Stop

Fashion Best & Best

Suzie Bag Nari Anna

Chris & Carol Apparel

1 Style in USA

TCEC

Nadia

AGP Apparel

Azules

107 SneakPeek

American Fit

2NE1 Apparel

J.R.B. Collection

Active Basic

JC & JQ

Mustard Seed

Fashion Love

Zexi

Coveted Clothing

Aryeh

SNS

5TH CULTURE

American Able

1 MAD FIT

DNA

LA SCALA

G-Gossip Apparel, Inc

Minuet

Anemone Urban X

T-party

Moa Collection

Voll

Huncho

17 Young Dress

Signature 8

YoYo5

Cherish

ShoeMaiden by Glamoure

Clothing Company

AppleJuice

Accessories by Glamoure

ZENANA

Fornia Apparel

Do + Be Collection